Copyright © 2016 Hawk's Nest Publishing, LLC
Cover and internal design © 2016 by Sourcebooks, Inc.
Illustrations by Natalie Thomson
Cover design by The Book Designers
Internal design by Travis Hasenour/Sourcebooks
Cover and internal images © shutterstock/Paul Crash, shutterstock/Seregam, shutterstock/Elliotte Rusty Harold, shutterstock/Sergio33, Thinkstock/blue67sign

Sourcebooks and the colophon are registered trademarks of Sourcebooks, Inc.

All rights reserved. No part of this book may be reproduced in any form or by any electronic or mechanical means including information storage and retrieval systems—except in the case of brief quotations embodied in critical articles or reviews—without permission in writing from its publisher, Sourcebooks, Inc.

All brand names and product names used in this book are trademarks, registered trademarks, or trade names of their respective holders. Sourcebooks, Inc., is not associated with any product or vendor in this book.

Published by Sourcebooks Jabberwocky, an imprint of Sourcebooks, Inc.
P.O. Box 4410, Naperville, Illinois 60567-4410
(630) 961-3900
Fax: (630) 961-2168
www.sourcebooks.com

Source of production: Versa Press, East Peoria, Illinois, USA
Date of production: April 2016
Run number: 5006380

Printed and bound in the United States of America.
VP 10 9 8 7 6 5 4 3 2 1

LET'S COLOR!

TOTALLY MICHIGAN!
A TOTAL SECRET!

Use the key to decode the message.

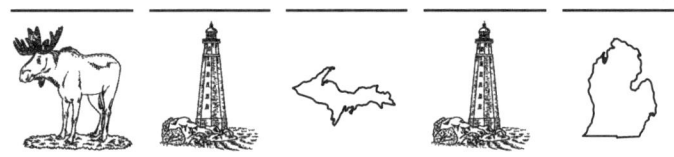

KEY

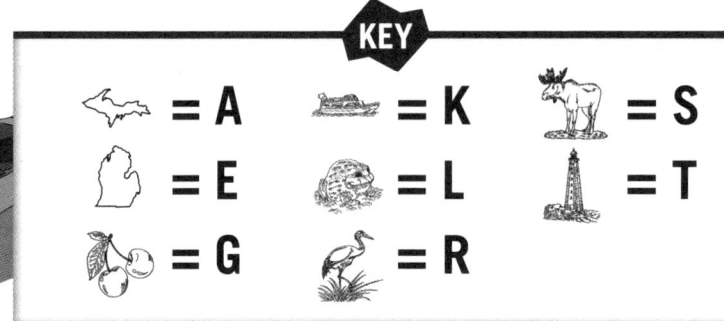

Solution is on page 51.

LET'S SOLVE!

Help the kayaker cross the straits into Mackinac Island.

Solution is on page 51.

TOTALLY MICHIGAN!
TOTALLY SCRAMBLED!

Unscramble the letters of these items found near the **GREAT LAKES**.

ACREN

TBSALIAO

_ _ _ _ _

RFRYE

TULGIEOSHH

_ _ _ _ _ _ _ _ _ _

YKKAA

MHRENFIAS

_ _ _ _ _ _ _ _ _

Solution is on page 52.

LOST IN MICHIGAN!

```
O W S W A N I R S B H
U R B U A M R K Y U M
I R R A P S O V Z G A
B T I H B E A C H N W
K T D I E R R N F X Z
G A G H S I S I F W H
F A E M U E V N O N G
V R Q X Y R D A T R B
L I G H T H O U S E O
M I C H I G A N N L V
P X C Q W T S Z A E T
```

BEACH
BRIDGE
DUNE

ERIE
HURON
LIGHTHOUSE

MICHIGAN
SUPERIOR
SWAN

Solution is on page 52.

TOTALLY MICHIGAN! CROSSWORD PUZZLE!

◀ ACROSS ▶

3. Lake _____ is north of the Upper Peninsula and reaches all the way to Canada.

6. The states of _____ and Ohio are side by side on the southern border of Michigan.

7. The largest city in Michigan is _____.

8. _____ is the state capital of Michigan.

DOWN

1. The _____ Bridge connects the Lower Peninsula and the Upper Peninsula.

2. The four Great Lakes that border Michigan are Lake Erie, Lake _____, Lake Michigan, and Lake Superior.

4. The state bird of Michigan is the American _____.

5. The Lower Peninsula is shaped like a _____.

Use your knowledge of **MICHIGAN** culture to solve the puzzle.

Hint! This bridge is named after a famous Michigan island!

Solution is on page 53.

TOTALLY MICHIGAN! LET'S MATCH!

Choose a **MICHIGAN** city or landmark from the word bank and write it on the corresponding line.

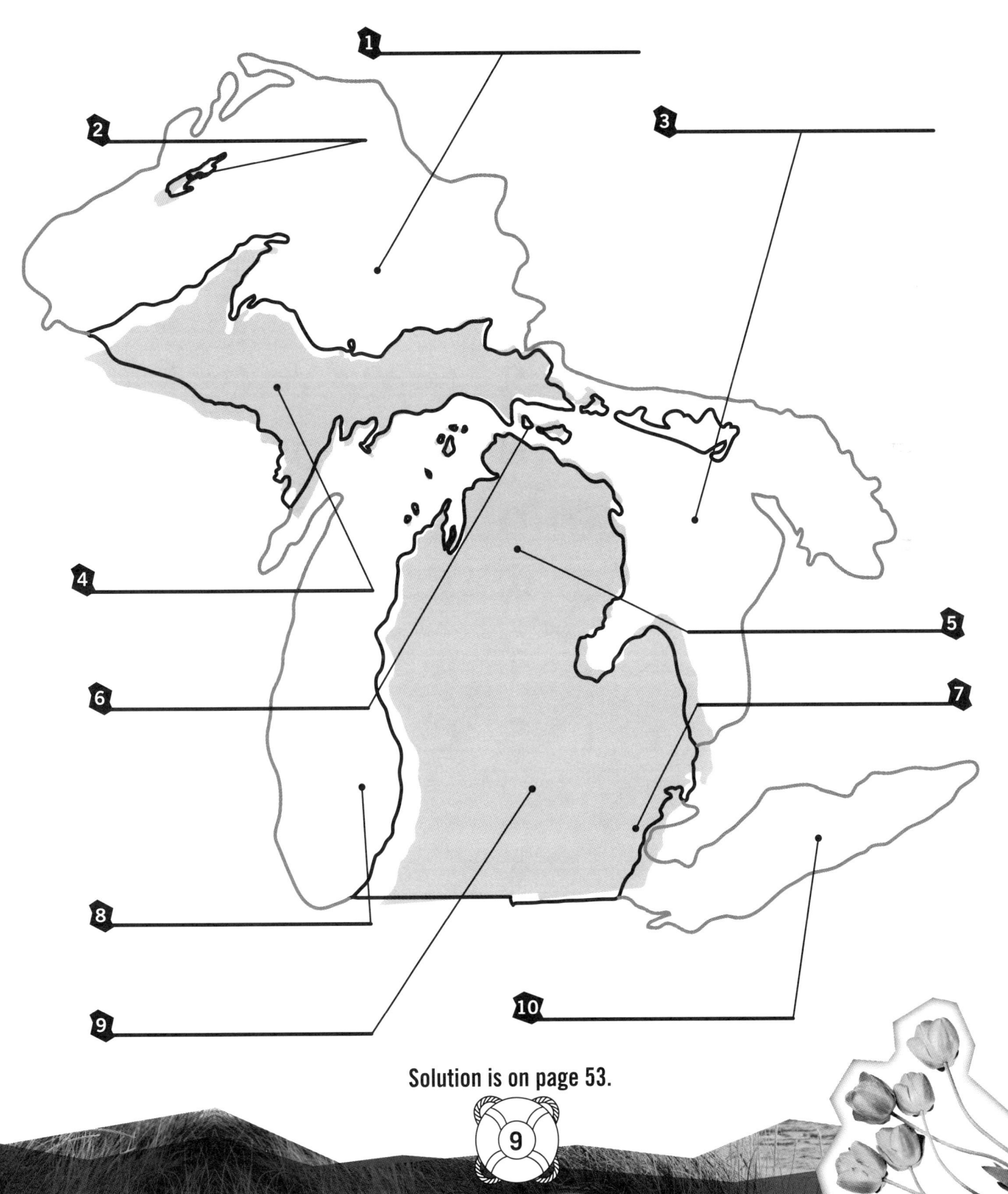

Solution is on page 53.

TOTALLY MICHIGAN!
LOST IN MICHIGAN!

```
H G T M A C K I N A C
M P D H V A I A A M I
B E E G F U D G E M G
F N M T F T T Y T O H
U I B C O O Q O J T B
I N O H O S G O Y O F
S S Z T T H K P U R M
G U T W B O N E E C Z
I L I I A W T R Y I V
E A G M L T A S Z T L
T R O L L S C F N Y H
```

AUTO SHOW	MACKINAC	PETOSKEY
FOOTBALL	MOTOR CITY	TROLLS
FUDGE	PENINSULA	YOOPERS

Solution is on page 54.

LET'S DRAW!

Use the grid to draw a sandhill crane.

TOTALLY MICHIGAN!
FOLLOW THE PATH!

Which ferry is headed to Mackinac Island?

Solution is on page 54.

FIND THE DIFFERENCES!

Can you find all three differences between the Mackinac Bridge images below?

Solution is on page 54.

TOTALLY MICHIGAN! CONNECT THE DOTS!

A TOTAL SECRET!

Use the key to decode the message.

W A T E R

W O N D E R L A N D

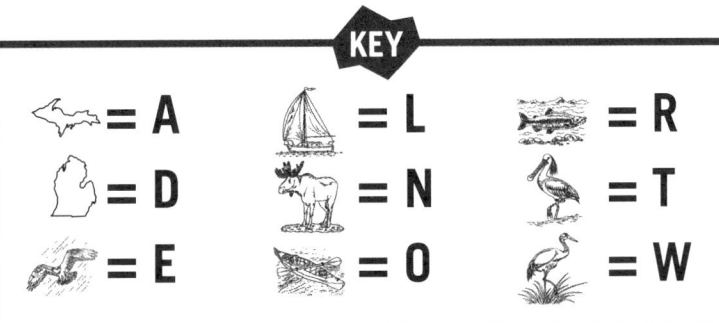

KEY

- = A
- = D
- = E
- = L
- = N
- = O
- = R
- = T
- = W

Solution is on page 55.

TOTALLY MICHIGAN! HIDDEN PICTURE!

Use the key to color the shapes below and reveal the hidden picture.

A = Black
D = Yellow
B = Brown
E = Blue
C = Green
G = Grey

Hint! Color inside the lines!

A MICHIGAN DOODLE!

Who is surfing down the Sleeping Bear Dunes?

Hint! Use your imagination!

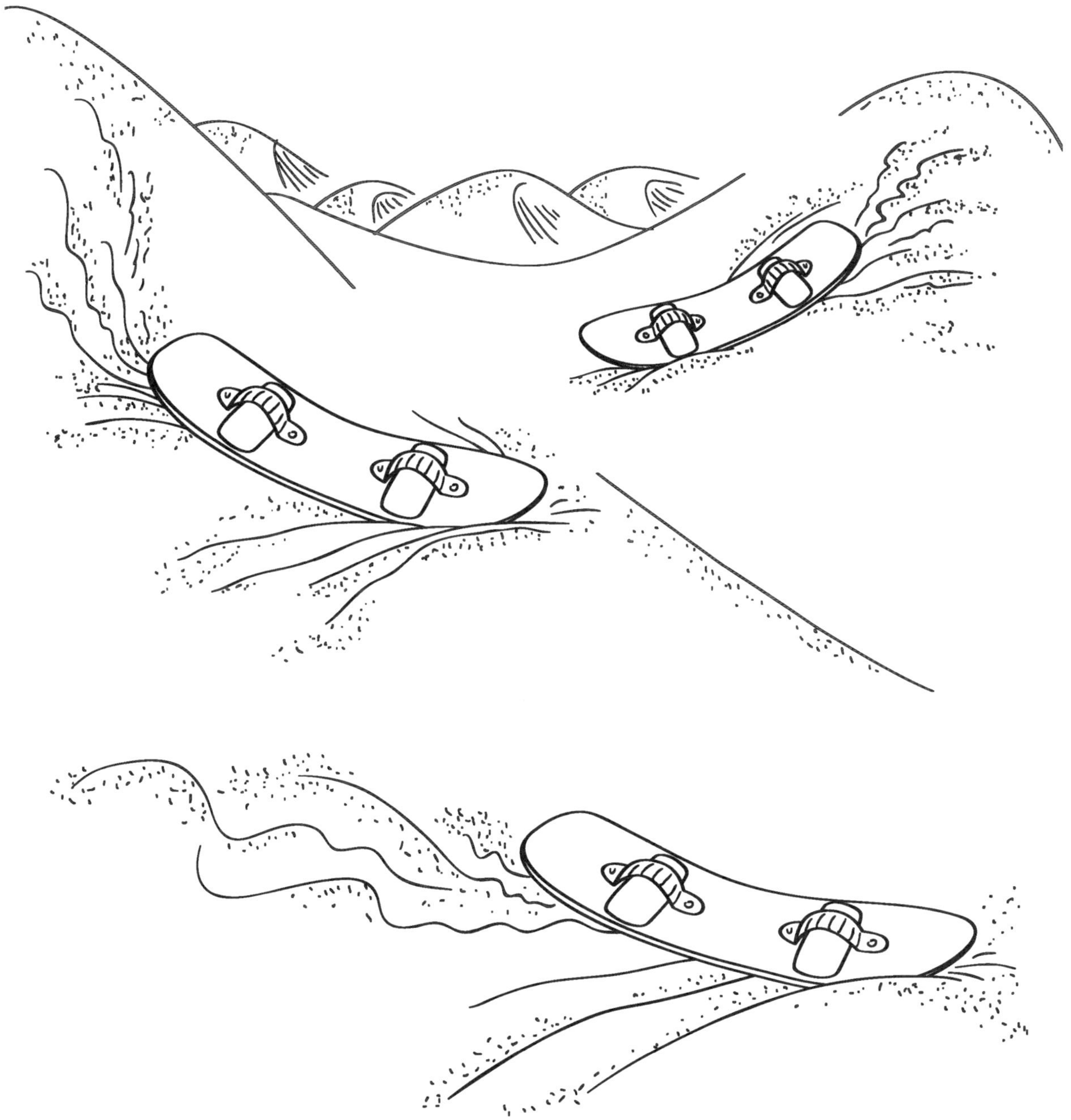

TOTALLY MICHIGAN! CROSSWORD PUZZLE!

◀ ACROSS ▶

1. Don't leave Mackinac Island without enjoying some famous homemade _____!

4. Frankenmuth is famous for fried _____ dinners.

6. Battle Creek, Michigan is the home of a major manufacturer of this crunchy breakfast food.

8. _____ is a popular brand of soda pop in the peninsulas, locally headquartered in Detroit.

DOWN

2. Vernor's _____ Ale is a local Michigan favorite.

3. The Traverse City _____ Festival is named for this small, red, round fruit.

5. You can enjoy a piping hot stuffed meat pie called a _____ in the U.P.

6. "Superman" flavored ice _____ is a combo of three colors: blue, red, and yellow, just like the super hero!

7. The "Coney Island" hot _____ or "Coney" is a Michigan specialty.

Use your knowledge of **MICHIGAN** foods to solve the puzzle.

Solution is on page 55.

TOTALLY MICHIGAN!
TOTALLY SCRAMBLED!

Unscramble the letters of these animals found in the Upper Peninsula!

KBLCA AERB

__ __ __ __ __   __ __ __ __

OMOES

__ __ __ __ __

TTREO

__ __ __ __ __

FLLGBORU

__ __ __ __ __ __ __ __

PIANGSPN ERTTUL

__ __ __ __ __ __ __ __   __ __ __ __ __ __

XLNY

__ __ __ __

Solution is on page 56.

TOTALLY MICHIGAN!
LOST IN MICHIGAN!

```
G E B Y E S N P F R D M S
R T R A V E R S E C I T Y
A K V R T D L V R P P L H
N I A H O T K A Q P J W E
D B T L O F L I N T J B F
R E J C A L P E E S J B E
A R J F W M L Z C V I M B
P R D L T I A A S R J N Y
I A F V G Y U Z N I E E G
D E T R O I T Z O D I E L
S E O A N N A R B O R P K
```

ANN ARBOR   FLINT   KALAMAZOO
BATTLE CREEK   GRAND RAPIDS   LANSING
DETROIT   HOLLAND   TRAVERSE CITY

Solution is on page 56.

LET'S DRAW!
Use the grid to draw **MICHIGAN** cherries.

TOTALLY MICHIGAN!
LET'S SOLVE!
Where does the family go for vacation?

START HERE!

TULIP TIME FESTIVAL
HOLLAND, MI

NATIONAL CHERRY FESTIVAL
TRAVERSE CITY, MI

Solution is on page 56.

A TOTAL SECRET!

Use the key to decode the message.

F O R E V E R

W I L D

KEY

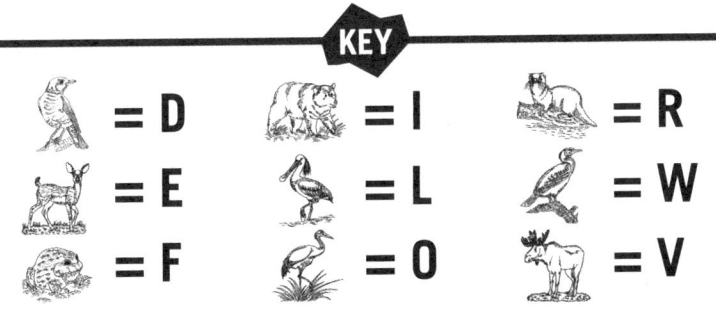

Solution is on page 57.

TOTALLY MICHIGAN!
LOST IN MICHIGAN!

```
D L W A T E R F A L L
J P U R A F T I N G W
F P R M X H O S Q N Q
I O V C B M A R X F G
S R R L O E P S E C L
H C V I P P R C Y S Z
I U X F Z L P J L Z T
N P C F L A X E A P M
G I U M D R H C R C P
S N O W M O B I L E K
Q E N T A R G Z B N I
```

CLIFF	FOREST	RAFTING
COPPER	LUMBERJACK	SNOWMOBILE
FISHING	PORCUPINE	WATERFALL

Solution is on page 57.

A MICHIGAN DOODLE!

Sled dog racing is a popular sport in the Upper Peninsula. What are these sled dogs pulling?

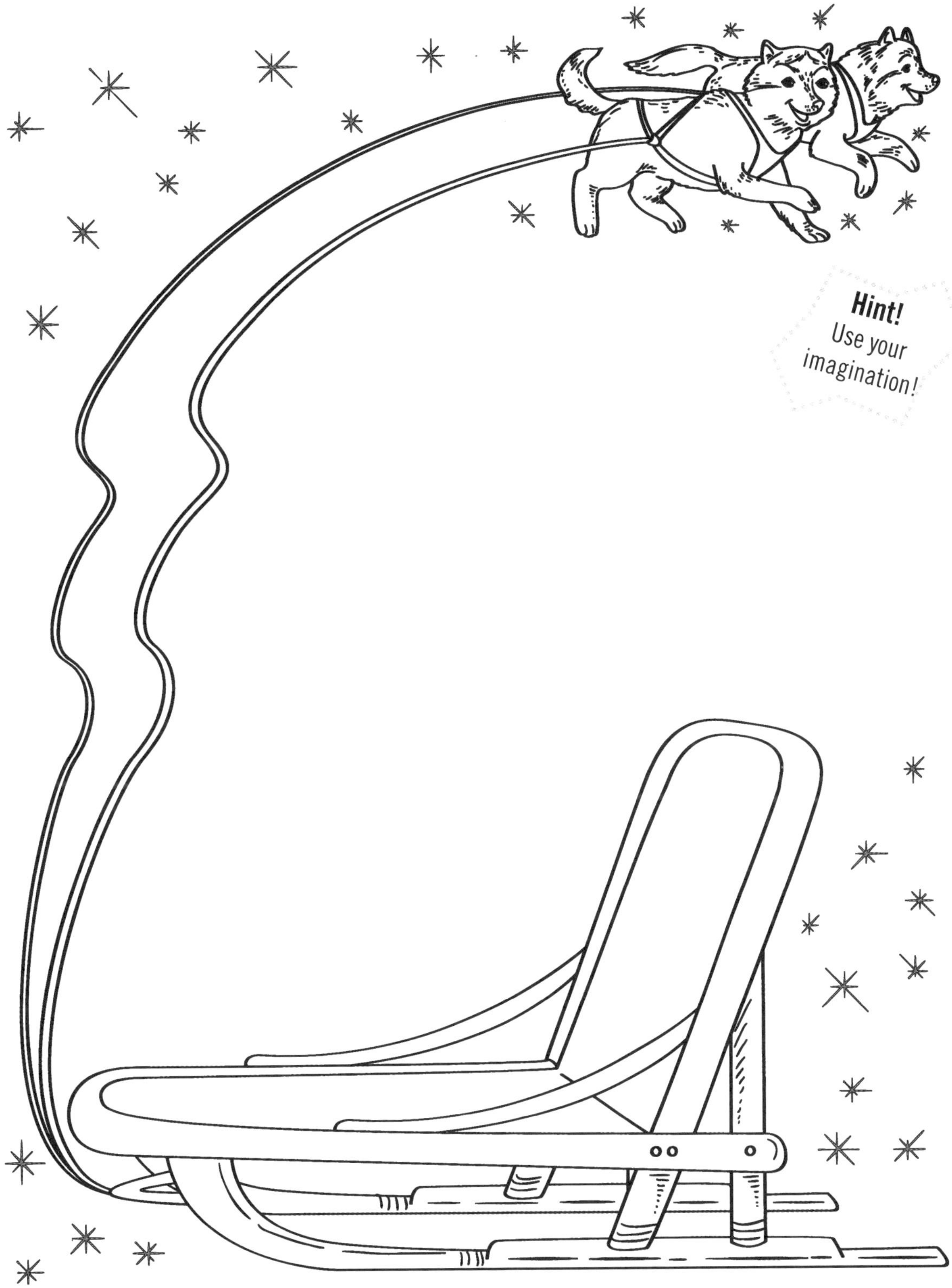

Hint! Use your imagination!

TOTALLY MICHIGAN!
WHAT'S IN A NAME?

How many words can you make using letters found in the three words below?

GREAT LAKES STATE

Example: RATE   TEE

1. _____
2. _____
3. _____
4. _____
5. _____
6. _____
7. _____
8. _____
9. _____
10. _____

11. _____
12. _____
13. _____
14. _____
15. _____
16. _____
17. _____
18. _____
19. _____
20. _____

Solution is on page 58.

TOTALLY MICHIGAN!
LOST IN MICHIGAN!

```
W F S O U T H H A V E N E
Q R I I V E I D R A G X Y
M B L A K E S H O R E S B
U U V D W A R C A D I A W
S B E P M C H Z C G B U C
K Z R E I Z X Q Y T Y G G
E S L E E P I N G B E A R
G C A C J A F G V I K T E
O P K S O R M C P S W U W
N K E F H K J N W V M C K
S O O L O C K S E C I K S
```

ARCADIA PARK SLEEPING BEAR
LAKESHORE SAUGATUCK SOO LOCKS
MUSKEGON SILVER LAKE SOUTH HAVEN

Solution is on page 58.

TOTALLY MICHIGAN! LET'S MATCH!

Match the sport with its corresponding gear.

FISHING

KAYAKING

SAILING

HOCKEY

WHITE WATER RAFTING

HIKING

CYCLING

Solution is on page 58.

A TOTAL SECRET!

Use the key to decode the message.

DETROIT

IS

MOTOR CITY

KEY

mitten = C, old car = E, city = O, boat = T
sports car = D, truck = I, UP = R, tulips = Y
bridge = M, cherries = S

Solution is on page 59.

TOTALLY MICHIGAN!
CONNECT THE DOTS!

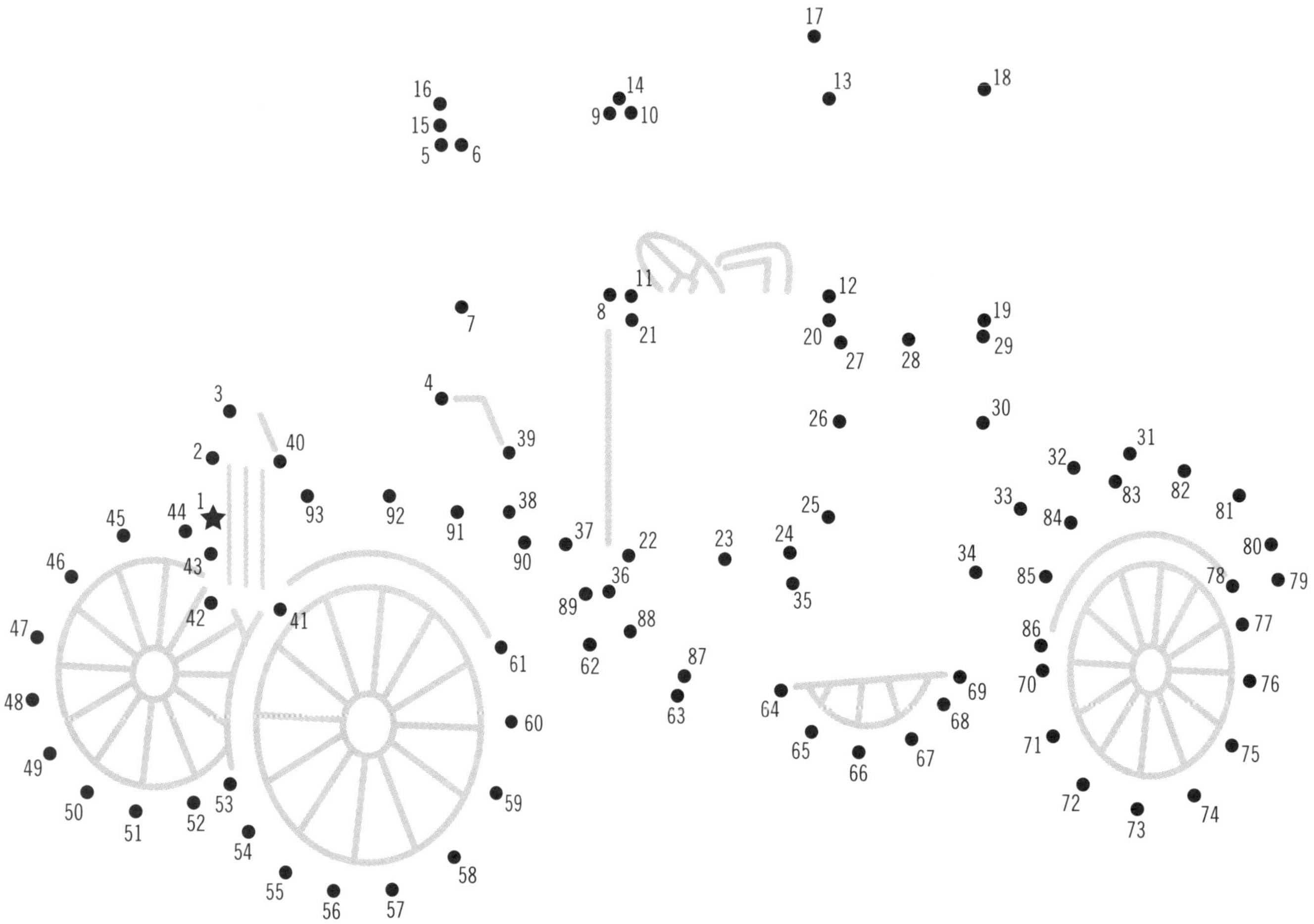

TOTALLY MICHIGAN! CROSSWORD PUZZLE!

◀ ACROSS ▶

5. _____ Park is the name of the Detroit Tigers ballpark.

7. The University of Michigan colors are blue and _____.

8. The NFL team that calls Detroit home is the _____.

DOWN

1. Al, the purple _____, is a mascot for the Detroit Red Wings.

2. The University of Michigan football team is called the _____.

3. NFL quarterback Tom _____ played college football at the University of Michigan.

4. Tennis superstar Serena _____ was born in Saginaw.

6. The Detroit _____ won the NBA Championship in 1989, 1990, and 2004!

Use your knowledge of **MICHIGAN** culture to solve the puzzle.

Hint! This animal has eight slippery legs!

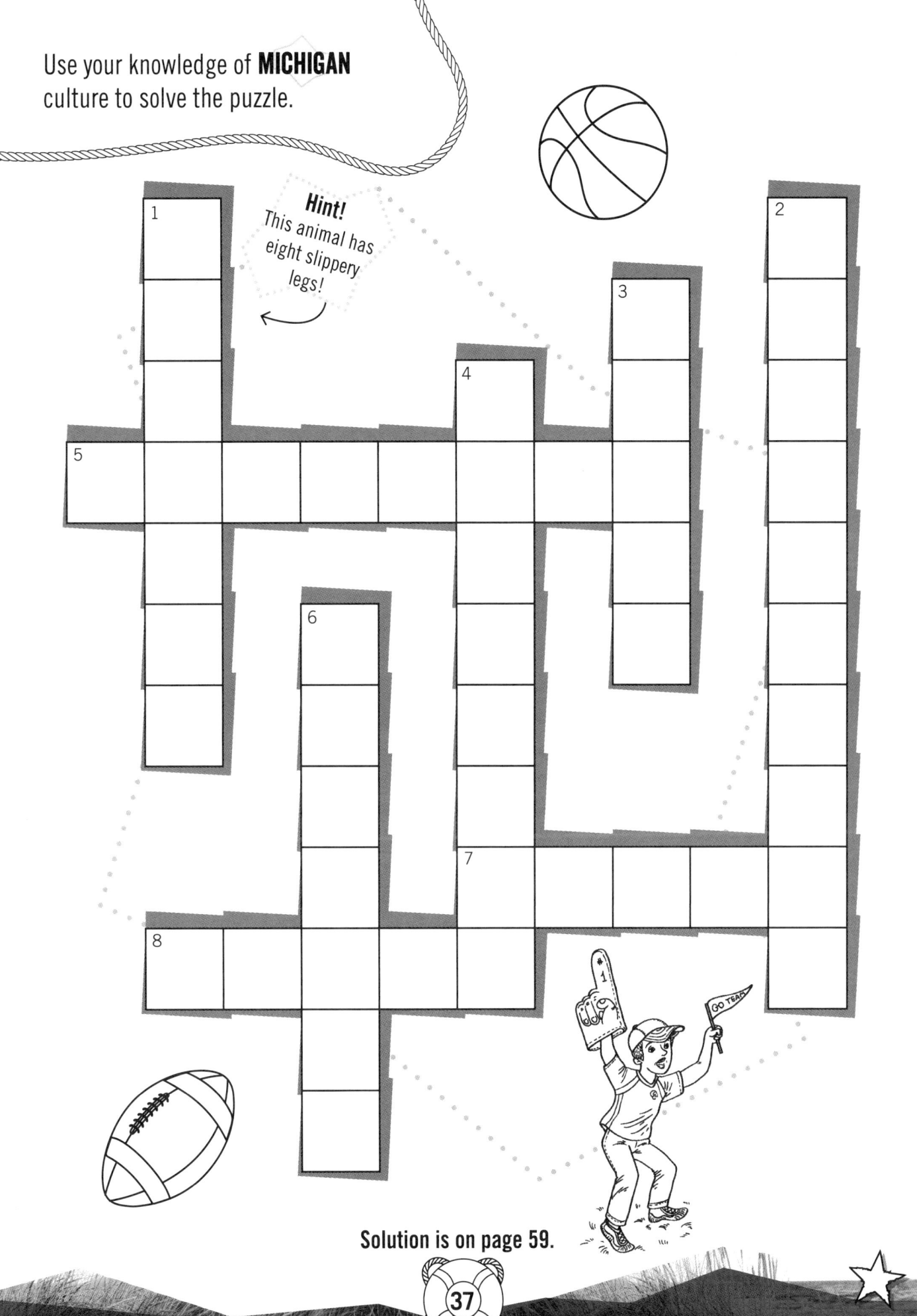

TOTALLY MICHIGAN!
TOTALLY SCRAMBLED!

Unscramble the letters of these **MICHIGAN** sights!

RCEYRH RETE

_____ ____

GRBIED

_____

EOMDL T

_____ _

ZJZA NADB

____ ____

ERATG SAKLE

_____ _____

NSAD UDSEN

____ _____

Solution is on page 60.

LOST IN MICHIGAN!

```
G B O W L S B T N C W M
W T R O P J H I O S X E
L O X L I E G G G A L Q
Q M X V S A B E G T G M
B X E E T P R R U R E E
B U M R O W A S D S K N
H M Y I N M J R N U U G
X N Z N S X X Y T F M Y
C O M E R I C A P A R K
A X C S T O F L I O N S
K L G S R E D W I N G S
```

BIG TEN
BOWLS
COMERICA PARK

LIONS
PISTONS
RED WINGS

SPARTANS
TIGERS
WOLVERINES

Solution is on page 60.

TOTALLY MICHIGAN!
LET'S SOLVE!

Help the white-tailed deer make it back to the forest.

START HERE!

Solution is on page 60.

FOLLOW THE PATH!

Which car is headed to Comerica Park for the baseball game?

Solution is on page 61.

TOTALLY MICHIGAN!
TOTALLY SCRAMBLED!

Unscramble the letters of these professional **MICHIGAN** sports teams.

STIPSON

___ ___ ___ ___ ___ ___ ___

SLOIN

___ ___ ___ ___ ___

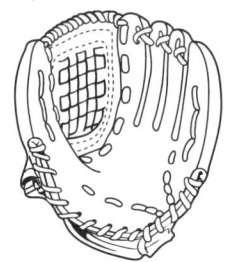

SUTNULG

___ ___ ___ ___ ___ ___ ___

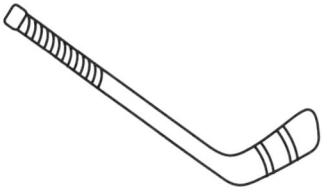

DER GWINS

___ ___ ___   ___ ___ ___ ___

GERTIS

___ ___ ___ ___ ___ ___

MIRALADS

___ ___ ___ ___ ___ ___ ___ ___

Solution is on page 61.

LET'S DRAW!

Use the grid to draw the sports car.

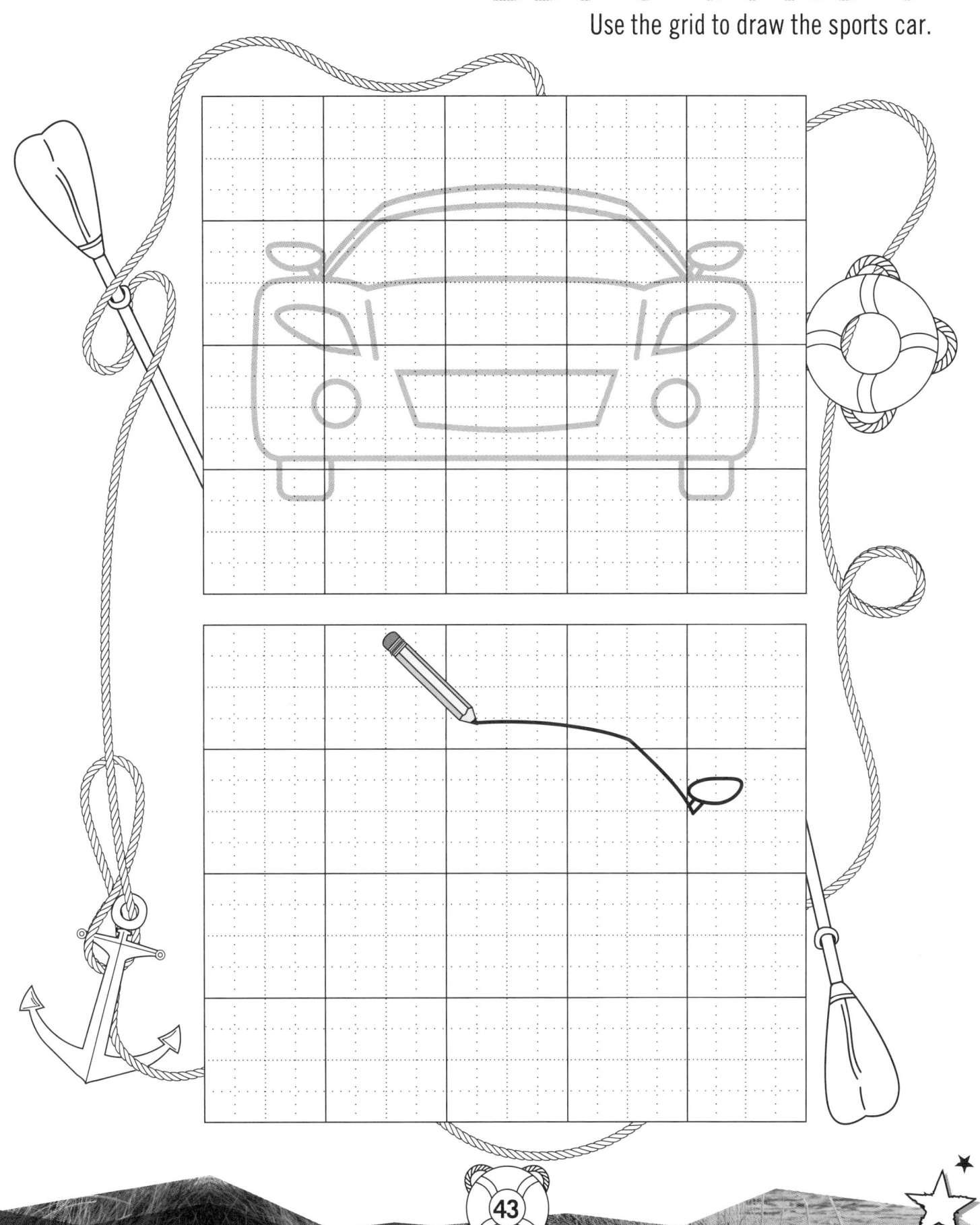

TOTALLY MICHIGAN!
CONNECT THE DOTS!

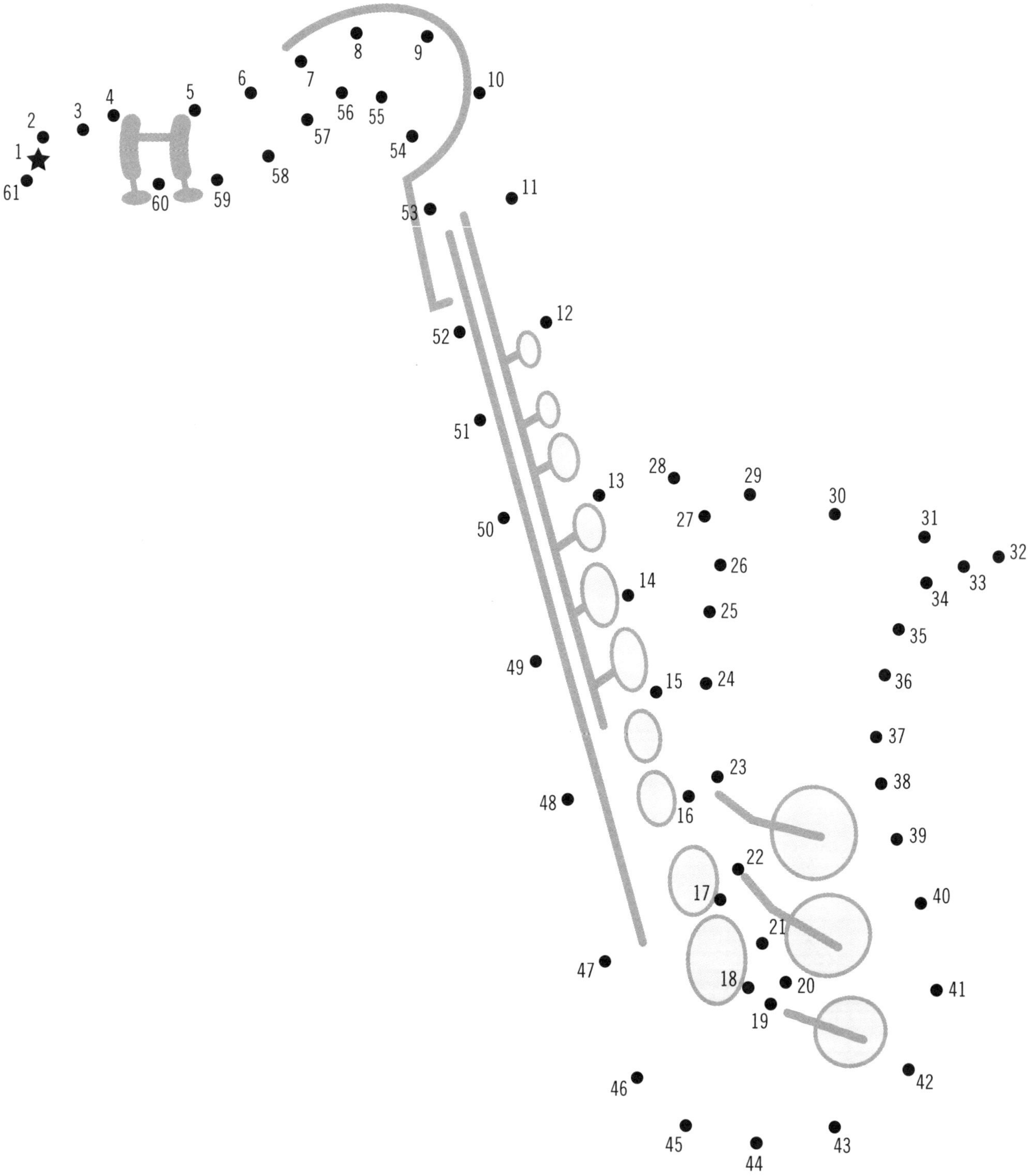

TOTALLY MICHIGAN!
LOST IN MICHIGAN!

```
Z T E M P T A T I O N S
N M U Q S E A M U V U O
S U P B K O B M H M F W
V S I M R O U J S O K I
F E A G A N A L I T U K
M U N L G D Y N T O Y K
F M O V P Y O E X W Z M
U E K G B T P N C N W G
S T E V I E W O N D E R
O U H Q G A L X P A I G
W H I T E G L O V E A Y
```

IGGY POP
MADONNA
MOTOWN
MUSEUM
PIANO
SOUL
STEVIE WONDER
TEMPTATIONS
WHITE GLOVE

Solution is on page 61.

FIND THE DIFFERENCE!

Can you find all three differences between the two images below?

Solution is on page 62.

TOTALLY MICHIGAN! CROSSWORD PUZZLE!

◀ ACROSS ▶

5. Isle Royale is the largest _____ in Michigan.

6. Michigan became the 26th _____ when it entered the Union in 1837.

8. Detroit, nicknamed "Motor City," is home to the American _____ industry.

9. The Straits of Mackinac divide Michigan into the _____ Peninsula and the Lower Peninsula.

DOWN

1. Former U.S. President Gerald R. _____ was a football star at the University of Michigan.

2. The Henry Ford _____ contains many exhibits featuring American ingenuity.

3. Michigan was originally colonized by this European nation.

4. The official nickname for the state of Michigan is the Great _____ State.

7. The University of Michigan is located in the city of Ann _____.

Use your knowledge of **MICHIGAN** cities to solve the puzzle.

Hint! Je t'aime Michigan!

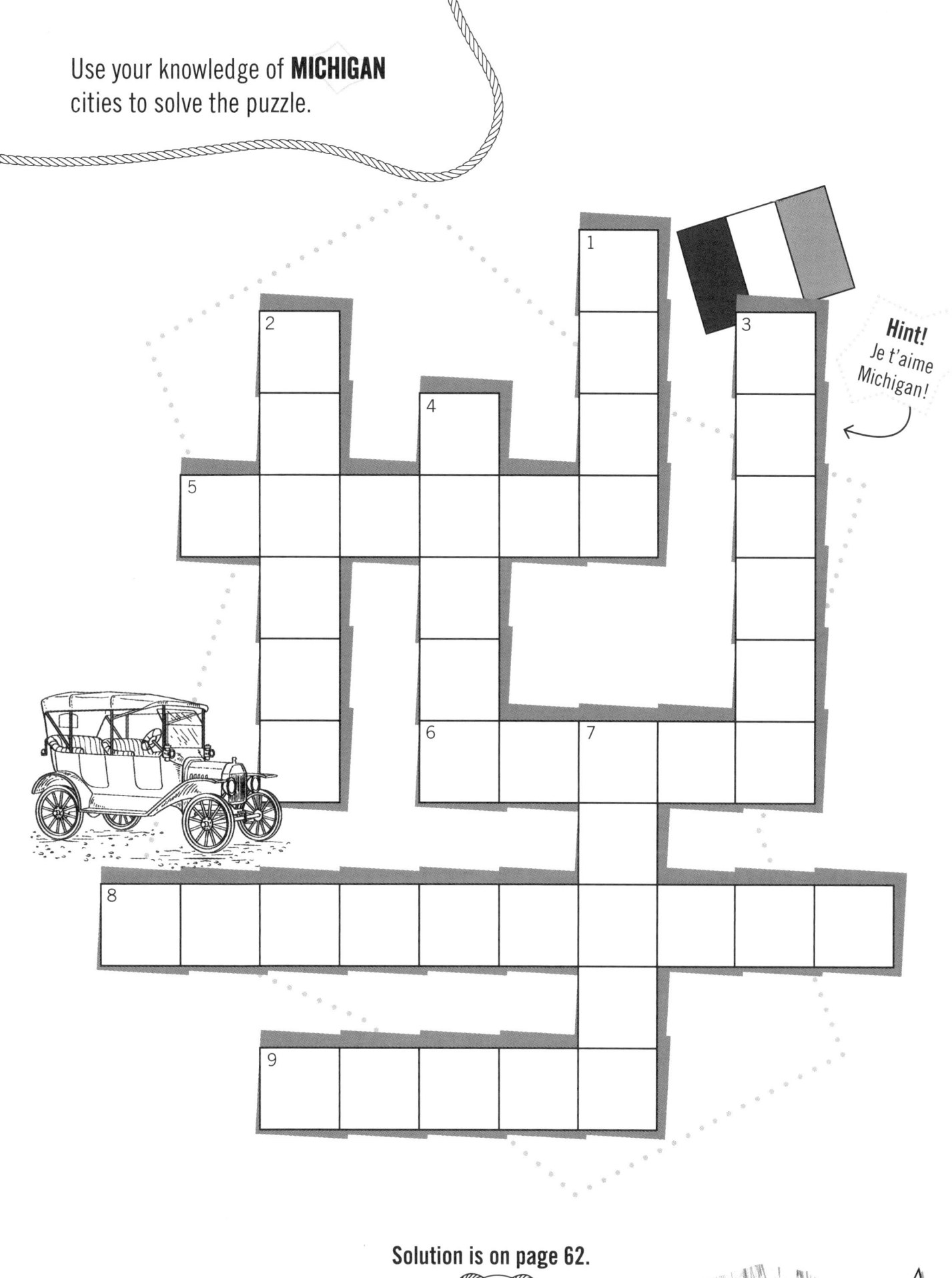

Solution is on page 62.

TOTALLY MICHIGAN!
A TOTAL SECRET!

Use the key to decode the message.

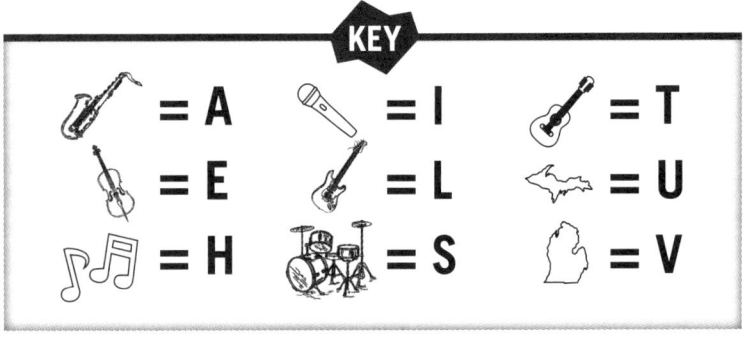

KEY

🎷 = A	🎤 = I	🎸 = T
🎻 = E	🎸 = L	◠ = U
🎵 = H	🥁 = S	⬢ = V

THANKS FOR VISITING
MICHIGAN

Solution is on page 62.

50

SOLUTIONS

Page 2

Page 3

Page 4

CRANE   SAILBOAT

FERRY   LIGHTHOUSE

KAYAK   FISHERMAN

Page 5

Page 7

Page 9

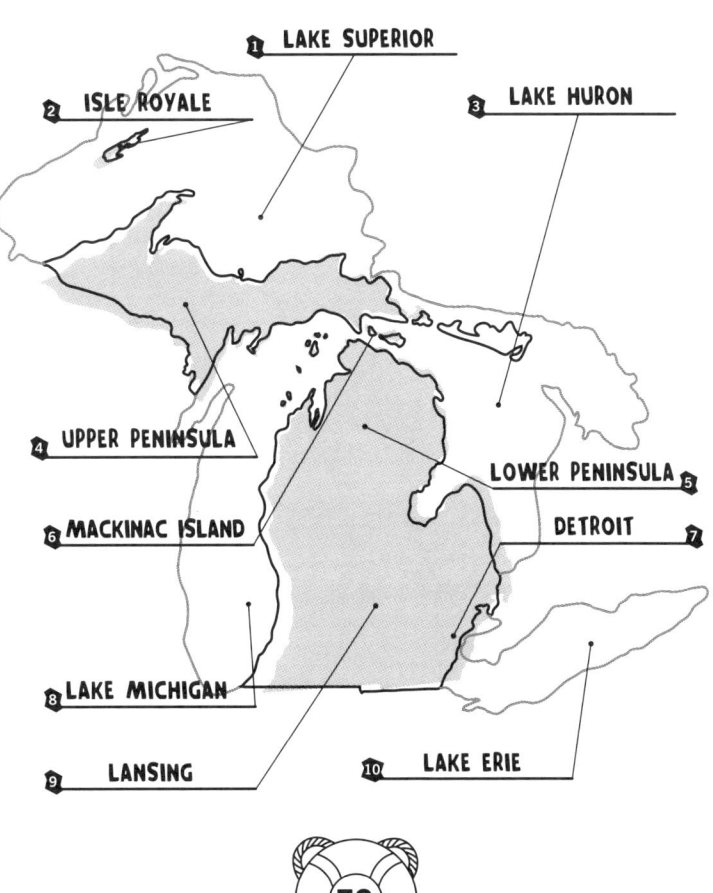

Page 10

Page 12

Page 13

Page 15

WATER

WONDERLAND

Page 19

Page 20

BLACK BEAR

MOOSE

OTTER

BULLFROG

SNAPPING TURTLE

LYNX

Page 22

Page 24

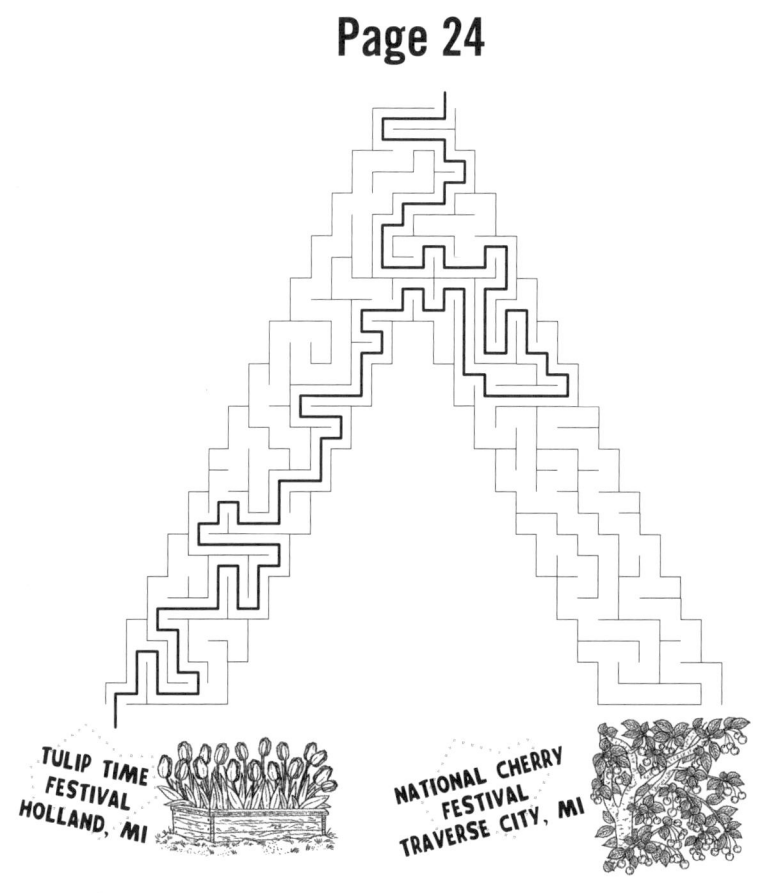

Page 25

FOREVER

WILD

Page 26

Page 28
Below are just a few examples of words that could be made with these letters.

GREAT LAKES STATE

age	estate	late	rest	stale	talk
agree	gas	leak	sage	stalk	tar
are	gate	lease	sale	star	tart
art	gel	letter	salt	start	task
ate	get	rag	seal	startle	tea
eagle	glee	rage	sear	steak	tee
ear	kettle	rate	seat	steel	test
earl	large	rattle	stag	take	treat
eat	last	relate	stage	tale	trek

Page 30

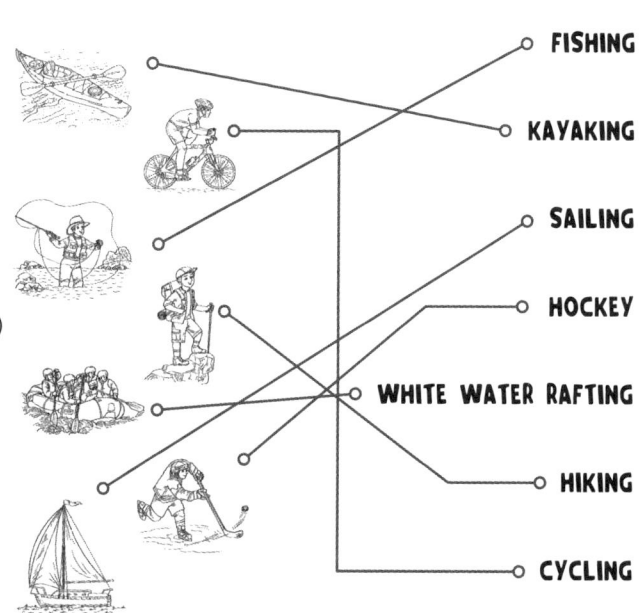

Page 32

Page 33

DETROIT

IS

MOTOR CITY

Page 37

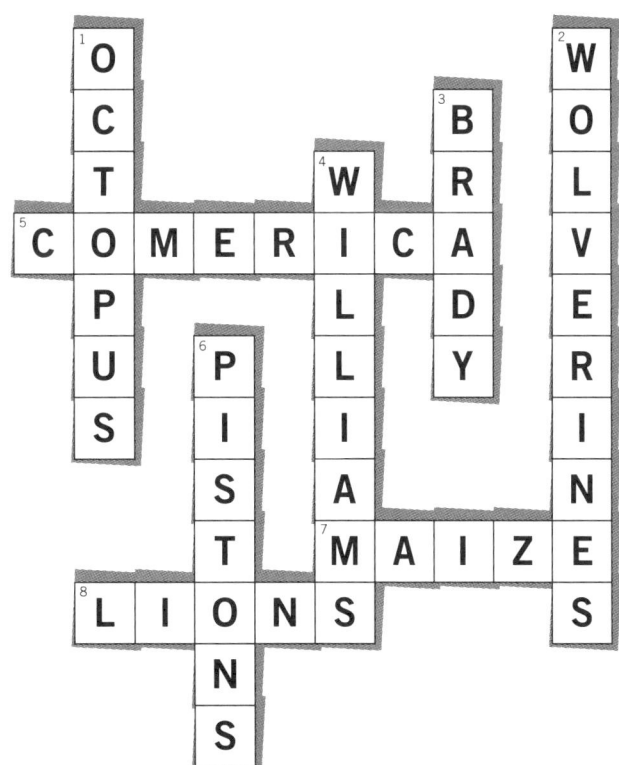

Page 38

CHERRY TREE

BRIDGE

 MODEL T

JAZZ BAND

 GREAT LAKES

SAND DUNES

Page 39

```
G B O W L S B T N C W M
W T R O P J H I O S X E
L O X L I E G G G A L Q
Q M X V S A B E G T G M
B X E E T P R R U R E E
B U M R O W A S D S K N
H M Y I N M J R N U U G
X N Z N S X X Y T F M Y
C O M E R I C A P A R K
A X C S T O F L I O N S
K L G S R E D W I N G S
```

Page 40

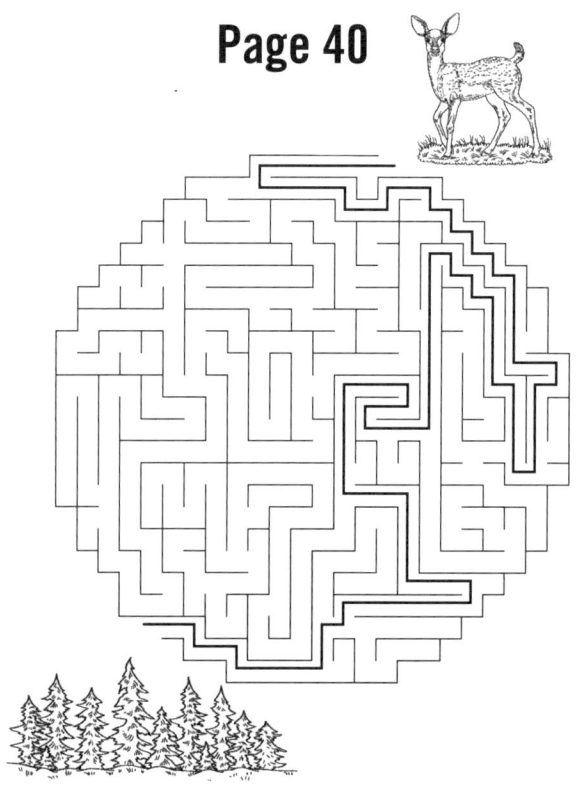

Page 41

Page 42

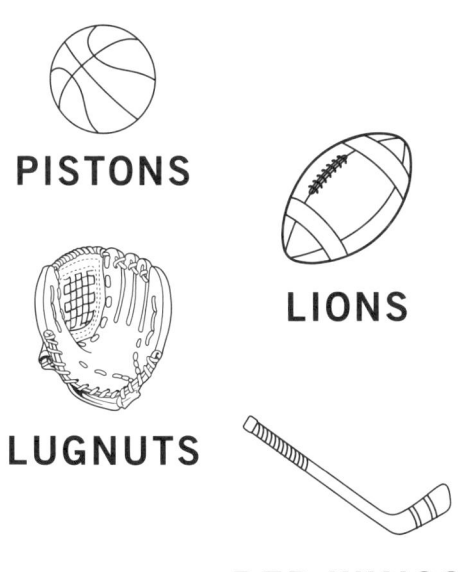

PISTONS

LIONS

LUGNUTS

RED WINGS

TIGERS

ADMIRALS

Page 46

Page 47

Page 49

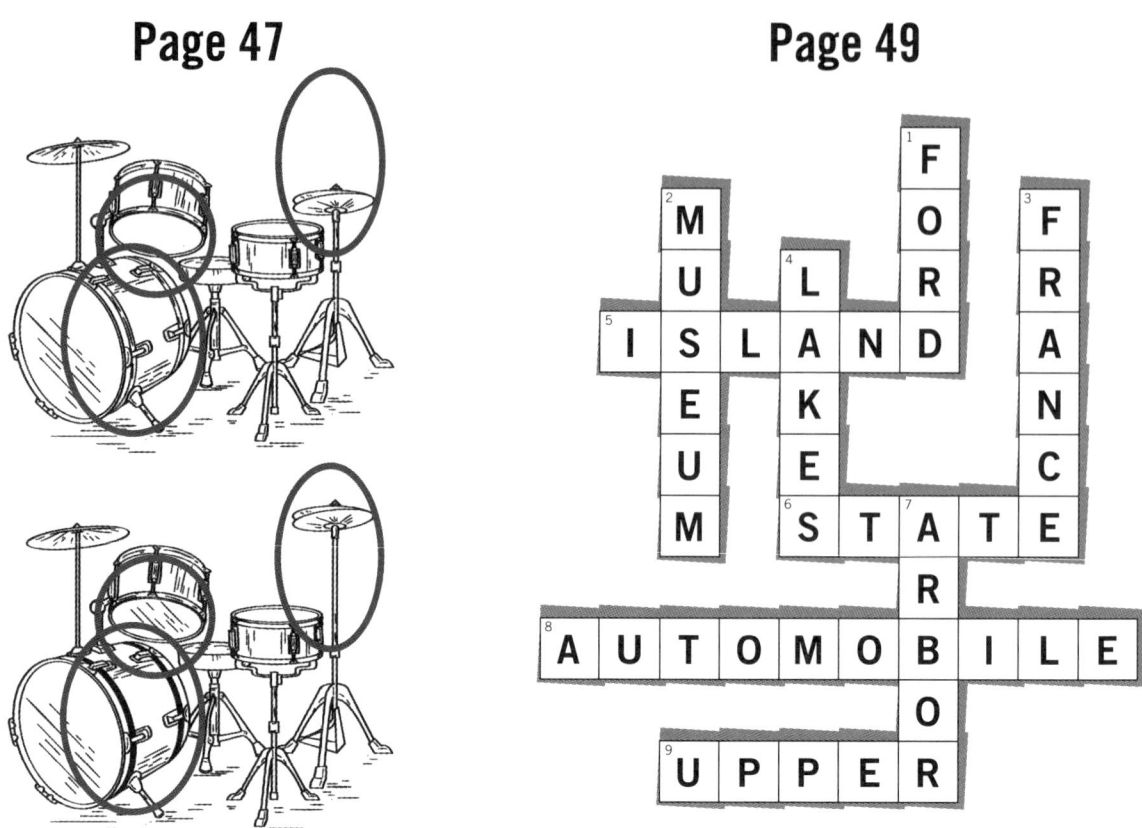

Page 50

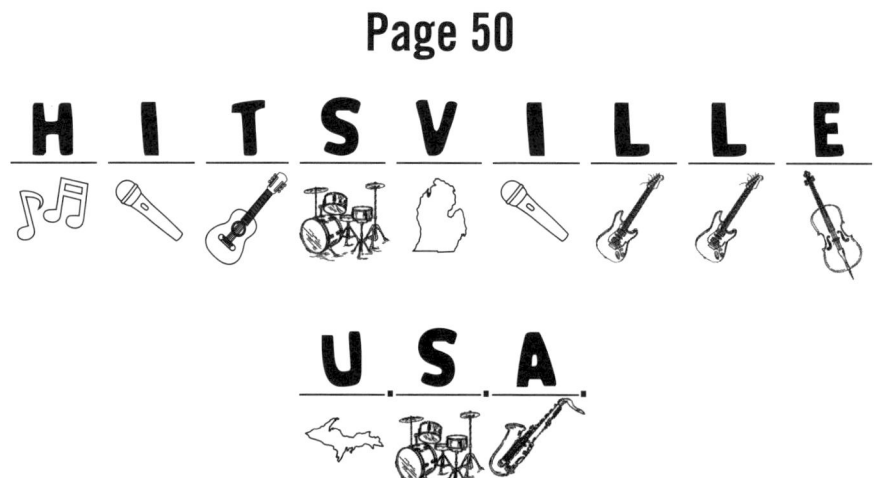